COLOR ME, LIFE'S POETRY

ALISON SEATON

Eternal Water Publications books may be ordered through Amazon.com or at: www.eternalwaterpublications.com

Eternal Water Publications LLC.
P.O. Box 880373 Port St. Lucie Florida, 34988

Cover image is provided by ©Istockphoto
Cover design by Miguel Hastings
eBook created with ePubTemplates.com

ISBN: 978-0-9968971-3-6

Printed in the United States of America
Printed by Create Space, an American Company

TABLE OF CONTENTS

Dedication

Foreword

Colors

Author's Notes

Acknowledgements

Dedication

To my Father and Mother,

Who encouraged me over the years and created in me an appreciation for the discipline and the art of writing. I have been inspired by your written work.

To my High School English Teacher-Mr. Brand wherever you are: Thank you for your inspiration and for taking my curiosity, dreams, drive, light and dark moments, and showing me how to give them life on paper.

Foreword

Color Me, Life's Poetry is a collation of impressions inspired by literature, popular culture, idioms, conversations with others, and the news. As you read please understand that the poems may possess several themes mirroring how different people feel or are inspired by the same color. Let each flash take you to their reflection point.

I encourage you to read the Author's notes to get a sense of each poem's background and general outline so no message gets missed. Keep in mind the themes arise from situations which are rarely mine. Avoid the temptation to think so.

Technically speaking, I am a budding poet learning my craft as I go. As such I attempt to explore a variety of forms. I am aware that because of my limitations the poems may not follow the accepted constructs. Secondary to that is the conscious attempt to use uncommon words which may have fallen to the wayside in our popular culture. There is a tendency these days to oversimplify things. While simplification is efficient there is also value in having and using a rich vocabulary. I believe when words are used well, writers address rich experiential layers otherwise uncommunicated without them. When this richness is lost to us the depth of our human experience suffers.

But most importantly I attempt to portray each color with the integrity needed for each impression to express itself clearly. Empathize as you share in each journey. We all can benefit from light shed on the painful, the comforting, the taboo, the romantic, the politically incorrect, or the socially and politically expedient. May you find joy and beauty in the experience of "Color Me" and be tolerant of my efforts.

COLOR ME, LIFE'S POETRY

ALISON SEATON

Colors

Black

Sparks dampen to ash in my mouth
Bitter sweet the pain sours then rocks
me to embrace myself. Hold it in or rout
it with gelatinous, big, globular, drops.
But there's no escaping the enveloping, disorienting, night.

Hemlock to joie de vivre
is missing the soft resiliency of your cheeks
as my fingers trace vers libre
stanzas fecund of love song till you weep
in ecstasy, a release of passion, too full to keep inside.

There's no reflection in this wallowing
Swallowing succubus - Noche de dolor.
All around everyone is dressed in it and talking
in stilted whispers. I cry por favor
for reprieve to Time, caught in the act of passing, deaf, impervious.

I hide in it waiting for the mood
to pass hoping to be a Phoenix
thankful for this masking cloak, covering bad and good.
Romulus killing Remus, Sabine stealing, this dark matrix
of deep sadness, through which I rise still screaming at your parting.

Yet there is nothing more elegant
than a Black Tie affair
White shirt gleaming like stacks of bleached bones
bound and fought over till by truce shared
between cummerbund and bow tie, themselves slaves to perfection.

All peripheral matter streams toward this.
None escape suffering, the center of influx, unable to break free
trapped, beleaguered then released with no instruction.
This road we all travel learning, self-taught invariably.
Choose pardon and light or accept acrimony and fade to inexorable
Black.

Green

Young buds and branches sat upon by Budgerigars
chirping, they with me, soak in the vibrant vernal sunshine.
Buoyant, my toes sink and soar through grass easily yar.
Springy, spongy, spiky soft, sensations sweeter than wine,
the tangy smell is airborne aft from the crush of my cuddled feet.

In the fen Swallows and Terns change guard with fireflies
flitting through the tall jade marsh grasses
rife with summer flowers.
I turn away to hotdogs, hamburgers, surf and sunscreen
but return to watch them again through mesmerized lashes

But fall is quiet and womblike in the forest
hushing my footfalls on fluffy folds of scrub.
To steady myself in the cocoon's induced drunkenness of solitude
I grasp moss dark verde carpeted trees for support
mourning with them the imminent loss of green

Emerald envelopes on postcards, cause envy of my visits to the Isles
Caribbean, Shamrock, Easter, Hawaii, and land of Mann
There a million shades of olive, lime, and bottle
rustle in the rainforest, verdant meadows and still woods
and I am reborn by the way they invigorate and calm me.

But the forests I traverse daily are lined by Presidents;
'Benjamins', McKinleys, Jacksons, Hamiltons and Grant.
Top drawer and canopy hold Madisons and secretary Chases.
Myself I find more often with Lincoln, Washington and some Jeffersons.
But their nature is strident, stark, military in operandi and unforgiving.

Brilliant iridescent cusp 'tween yellow and blue is the shade
that coats the princess Wicked and grows from a bevy
of resentments and avarice. Like bile bilious made
it wells from objective denied, obscuring the source to permeate
all thought till focus is only on acts of cupidity.
I do not mourn its passing when eliminated.
I can enjoy spring again.

When distilled to form you take shape as a child
stubbornly innocent of eye and heart, with arms open wide
to welcome the world.

Coquette, incorrigible, stormy, sleepy or wild
Insightful and fresh like cut crisp stalks of Celery and Romaine,
I will ever see the world through your eyes,
brimming with promise, never aging-
to unremittingly remain Green.

Grey

Harbinger of portents pending
premonitions osmose into me through the mist
I've heard tell of your exploits in my dreams
where every meaning is never as it seems
but revealed by Earl Grey vestiges, and bath salts after Sitz.

Between black and white exist excess of fifty shades.
Your stretched truths echo, excusing flaws
encompassing several hues. Silver satin spewed verbiage is nifty.
I search for veracity but drown in confabulation.
Its myriad masks hint at pain deep, debilitating, and raw
and an inability to trust me or yourself. So there's confrontation.

This brings a mood heavy as pregnant pewter-cotton cumulonimbus
caught in angst unable to deliver their deluge or hold more.
But there are rumblings like potatoes put putting playing limbos
with the lid. There will be a reckoning, sparks and trembling galore
and bitter tears shed. All we need is a catalyst- some tiny taper
or fagot I've nursed and hidden in my purse.
I promise I won't forget to arc it into your heart
made of tinder and pelt at you reducing us to vapor.
Your nemesis, lipstick-ed sheets, credit card slips, recorded dirty talk.

I'm left sitting, staring, twirling the wine glass
as the waiter removes the check and vanishes giving me space.
Relief, anger, pain, bitterness, wrestle in my chest and I declare an impasse.
The only thing you took care of with judicious grace
was the bill. I begin the journey back to myself with iron will.
But the walk is soaked in memories of you making me laugh and cry still.
Finally I am able see things differently and sleep through the night
The crazy daze of depression lifts and snowflakes of peace settle
patching up worn and empty spaces so I walk toward the light
thankful that this achromatic place is also found just before a sunrise.

Red

Sirens and squealing racecar wheels carry passengers
to put out or start fires with their passing.
There is something hot and smoky about a Fireman
holding his hose with tightened fingers
aimed at a fire. Blaze after blaze extinguished fully,
robbing death and decay of child, man, or woman.
He rallies others with tug, thrust, commands, and gushing sluice

Battlefield bravery is born from the same cloth.
To face what makes bleeders of us all, dread beast war's wroth;
inwardly or outwardly, and often forever,
and flinch not but forge on stoically to watch
friend or foe fall at your feet, rising again, never.
It's a job for kings and queens yet our youth we entrust.
And they come home to us, youth no more.

We help them as best we can to see through the haze
of pain, but cannot contain the outbursts of rage
that fester and linger creating collateral damage
because the inward bleed is a hemorrhaging mind beaten,
endlessly replaying the loop of violence and death, dazed.
It matters not that we are civilized.
Those words can't cover baseness of the human heart,
which constantly craves other people's goods.

Yet the crimson fields dotted with poppies or bleached crosses
do not opiate me from the scarlet flush of valentine roses
or the sweet spurt dripping down my chin from the crush
of my teeth through cherries. In your arms the rush
of heat flares anew each time you touch me
I feel your heartbeat strong and strident move speedily
to match mine in the throes of our lovemaking.
From this languorous sweetness I want to never be waking.

Afterwards, we savor the crumbling tart of raspberries
chased with crisp apple slices and frozen claret grapes
then sink lazily through red velvet topped with strawberries.
You guzzle great draughts of water before kissing my nape
returning to heat and rock us all over again.
The fire between us we effortlessly sustain.

4

Bad days are fire breathing dragons
where neither of us can miss a flaw, drawing blood
and I dive for cover from the darts you lob.
Do we need the draughts of water now? Where is the flagon
I wander as you march from the room and I start to sob?
At times I am relentless and you return home with flowers.
The storm passes and we forgive, eager to slake our thirst
for each other till a splash of carnelian taints the skies

Being with you is like seeing the startle of holly berries
amidst the green and hearing bells while kissing under mistletoe.
Vermillion ribbons shine fine and rare like Palo Cortado Sherry,
Ruby Nutcrackers line shelves, but unlike them our love is not for show
I am yours and you are mine and we hold hands
as we walk through the snow to Church.
Inside wafts the buttery smell of candles, red, white; their flames lurch
highlighting the blessing of us, and you twirl my wedding band

For Michael: blaze buster, soldier medic, my friend.

<u>Yellow</u>

Daffodils line the walkway to the garden,
I have run away with a theme and planted
Sunflowers, Buttercups and monochrome Iris' golden
hued amidst Blonde Gladiolus- by their beauty I'm blinded.
Mirroring sunshine the petals glow, so I bask, in never ending light.

Darling Dancer greets me daily with playful lick
and sits on my feet fully trusting and faithful-quick
to defend me in every situation.
He reminds me of you in our dating days- infatuation
blossoming to love too heavy and rich to keep clandestine
and so insidious it permeates every cell, a favorite tisane.

Ripening to reliability, love thudded in the blood beating place
growing from countless acts of knowing and being known
regardless of permutations, storms and haste, to a strong flow, never chaste.
I count on you - regular as Old Faithful, and on Dancer's happy groan

then, a burst of surprise quickens after the grey-
and we usher in burgeoning passion- no yellow-bellied stone!
Fervor hidden, under the surface, suddenly goes the geyser's way.

I melt as a result like a dollop of rich creamery butter
covering, crisp canary corn kernels completely.
Because what we have is sunshine- it matters
how we handle it. Too much burns and withers,
but just right, the heat, oh baby baby, yeah baby!

The couple next door is not so constant
neither do they photosynthesize positive energy.
Pusillanimous people; the husband, to his role is recreant
because fears flummox and anger stultifies yielding lack of spine.
He hits her and she stays yet about each other they whine.

You are my amber waves and favorite happy.
I would travel the cosmos, wait generations, for you
because you run through my veins zapping and zinging, electrically.
The magic between us cures my ennui
I crave you, breathe you, and you require and heed me,
together, we'll stay till the sun shines nevermore

Blue

Wispy clouds, scudding across earth's canopy highlight the brilliance
of the pastel hued water, lapping and slapping at my toes.
I slosh waist deep to you, open armed, lips puckered craving dalliance
but squeal as lifted aloft suddenly you dunk me, and so it oft goes.
Later, I lazily trail my hand down your back till you shiver.
One glance from you promises tonight you will make me quiver,
and I cannot wait, liquid and churning as the sea

It's refreshing not to have to hide how I feel
or coach speech into correct phrases you will accept
like my ex who spent hours controlling, making me reel
with insecurity while stealing away to kiss another - adept
at the lies. I love it when we can dance this way.
On vacation, we visit many places enjoying the splay
of light as it hits the ground, water, and each other's eyes.

The rhythm and hue of a Detroit band speaks easy to my soul
beat after beat interspersed between poignant melodies
weaving tapestries in song, and we dance and coil
about each other. Lost in vibrant strains the sweet remedies
pound stress away from my mind, surf to sand.
Gently, afterwards, we slow dance to a set
of refrains 'new and lean', sung melancholy by a Louisianian.

Gone are the days when I would hold up inside with a book
refusing to socialize piling up twisted tissues, lumpy with tons of tears
And, you sat watching reruns eating pizza washed down with Coke.
Our rise from these cobalt chains was dotted with rock of Gibraltar
nightmares
and revelations that chipped away at our faults.
The experience allowed us the tolerance to connect when we met
and I am truly grateful for you and you for me, our past cached in vaults.

We are luxurious deep indigo, navy, royal
and priceless. Nothing, not even time can separate us
from trust's ties. Being über loyal
we return to each other as to Capistrano the Swallows
and are forever bonded, religiously; skin to sinew.
The picture others get is reminiscent of Swans
necks arched about each other, forever gazing into souls renewed-
reflecting perfect white and perfect azure, elegant
amidst the backdrop of lapping gentle timeless ripples.

Dedicated to 'Thomas': your favorite color, my Halley's Comet.....

<u>White 1</u>

Picket fences, Plantation Shutters,
Closed closet doors have nothing on you
expert at denying, denigrating or ignoring
my feelings and existence when mad.

The glare of your chiseled gaze chills,
and I am confused yet certain
I will never breach the walls
to reconnect your heart to mine.

What is between us is thick

as the midwinter blizzard I slogged through
tonight, after parking three blocks down
in the only available spot.

Stumbling, past misshapen landmarks vaguely
like their real selves, matching memories
of how they used to look with the shadows;
phantoms, like the recollection of us
when we walked by them together so long ago.

A million pages of our story, each chapter unique
flutter by me falling softly and quietly
inexorably, onto the dusty ground
salted with tears and intentions gone awry.

My iced heart thaws suddenly in a torrent of tears
which I silently smother in the snowy pillow
until the echo of my shaking shoulders remains
leaving a taut pain lodged between burdened blades.

I acknowledge the shattering, helpless.
Fatigued from the fight
and countless shared failures
I fall asleep.

White 2

Light creamy wisps of cotton candy billow for miles
porous yet thick enough to jolt, shake and tilt
our weightless plane thirty thousand feet up.
While others read I gaze out the window
at startling pristine rows neatly marching in procession
mimicking 'on sale' racks of communion dresses.

When we get home laughs of pure delight escape us
when fluffy puffs, cotton ball and drift down just
as the hole rips mid pillow fight
and that same weightlessness reappears
when jumping and falling on the bed
amidst wafting curds.

Next evening, the flurry of balls bombard me,
missile missives of your playfulness,
released swiftly outside after the pre-spring storm.
And when I begin to win, you lay back making angels
sheer joy embodied in flapping your wings.

After you go inside the expectant hush
of myriad possibilities strike my mind
and bubbling heart. I survey snow laden fields,
ready canvas, computer screen, blank pad, vat of whipped cream.
How do I express all that is within
and do it justice, unfold the adventure with the telling?

White 3

Exuberant strains of the angelic host
chorus praise after Christ's birth. The spotless lamb
will bring us to our knees in His presence.
Blinding ivory, pearl, antique, alabaster
will emanate from the Light of ultimate Truth.
Redeemed we reign with Him forever,
in linen, Christ's bride, pure of heart,

Lavender

Will you walk with me to the creek today
and whisper to my heart endearments fey?
We'll sit on the banks and dangle our feet in ripples.
The dent, we rent in the water, sweet dimples.

Will you take my hand thread fingers through mine
gently stroking thumbs till tingles rill my spine?
Enthralled with your lips I lean close to kiss them
and find transport to treasure filled catechism.

Each kiss repeated reveals certain knowing
and more to know, my craving keeps growing.
You lay me down and hand me a posy
I sigh at your thoughtfulness glad I was choosy.

Lines bend the corners of your eyes when you smile
Lit with tender passion they beguile.
Please hold me thus beholden for a lifetime
to bask in the glow my heart echoes in mime.

Please walk with me to the creek today
I promise to whisper love in a million ways
that catch you up in ecstasy's endless eddies,
the waves, gentle miraculous remedies.

Take my hand, fingers entwine for more than a day
you said to me with your ring, this is for always.
At the creek, tears on my cheek I accepted your troth
My pledge, love and faithfulness forsooth

Garnet

If I could hold forgiveness in my hand
and offer it up to you without reprimand
would you take it and hold it to your breast too
till it soaked and worked its way through
the broken crevices in your worn tired heart
and life is restored to all withered parts?

I know it tries to beat strongly, unrestricted
and does a fair job but is obstructed
by guilt, shame, and pain slowly hemorrhaging
pitter patter pain, continuously dripping.
The ooze is primordial and congeals leaving scabs
you won't leave alone and at them dab.

I died for you seeing your wretched condition
shedding drops of garnet and generous carnelian.
Please take my free gift, hold it to your breast now
it works through the spirit; regenerates, renews
till cracked worn tired places are healed
Mind, soul, and spirit's guilt leave, un-relived

And after you do so, you will be reborn
and if sometimes you suffer, your heart's un-forlorn

10

priceless gems of my spirit you can anytime Mine
from the depths of my blood's engrafted lifeline
The beauty is you will then spread my free gift
living unfettered, other souls eternally lift.

<u>Copper 1</u>

Clouds rise in wisps from my morning cup a
steaming sleep's hold out of my cells.
Winter's fingers strangled the copper
neck of the shower making impotent the well.

They reach indolently past the cuff of
my slipper chilling the gentle swell
of my ankles. I shiver and read about the cop, her
chase of delinquents yielded spent shells.
They stole innocence from ladies copped a
feel, and performed acts on which the news dwells.

Finally up I move to cop a
squat behind my potter's wheel
generating my bread and butter,
profits pad my finances so they swell.

This piece though, a rich loamy copper
has been especially difficult to call well
It twists and turns a constant sickly flop of
sticky clay. I struggle to bring it to life, tell
the world what it wants, says the cup, huh?

When done it rests triumphant, cropped off
smoothen edges the patina of sunrise
on water labeled; Ariadne's Elixir in Copper.
People browse the gallery where it lies
And sip mugs of coffee made in Krups, Ahh!

Copper 2

The color of skin, hair, and foil rich soil
enflame us with passion. Copper
pennies, wire pipe and plumbing
snaking through walls, arm with your utility. Copper
Tiger's eye, red jasper and Venus's sign
enchant with your beauty. Copper
Ayurvedic medical instruments
bring me health, inspire with your versatility. Copper
alloy base of Brass and Bronze
bedazzle and bewitch with your brilliance. Copper
Jerusalem's temple gates
usher into the heavenly. Copper, rich Copper.

Brown

I bite with the gentle fervor of zealots
through **chocolate** chips, hot **fudge** gooey syrup
draped languidly over **seal brown** cake. Wrapping myself
in the milky musky velvet earth nut flavor
whose fumes tingle nerve endings – tantalizing, pleasure!
My morning Joe greets me strong and sweet.

Acolyte at the shrine of caffeine and **cocoa**
I marvel at the plethoric palette of **browns**
that these tonics and Earth have in common.
Café latte, caramel, nubuck, red ochre,
calming **sand** to passionate **sinopia**
From dust we are, a million high and low lights,
and to dust we will return.

The bolus from the earth erupts hot
and after cooling from **fulvous** and **rufous** colored liquid
sparks pale to **bole** then becomes charred **burnt umber**.
And like it our lifeline blazes fast and feisty
till age rattles foolhardiness out of our bones.
Life's lessons cataclysmic to the heart,
sharp, quick, and cloaked in steel, cut past bone to the meat of things.

The calm smooth **chamois** of wisdom
envelops those who've lived a little and learned a lot
buffing the spirit from **field drab** to resplendent **russet**.
The sword's swish from scabbard reveals the soul
burnished brilliantly, a blade ready and true.
Everyone forgets the symbiotic polishing
etched into the faithful casing- scabbard née flesh
nicked, scraped by thrusts and extractions of the volatile blade.
The spirit however, echoes in every whisper stroke through air
its mark indelible despite infinite invisibility

It will fly heavenward or to damnation

13

but regardless of residence will live forever,
From dust we are, a million high and low lights,
and to dust flesh will return.

Tin   (Tin Rhythm, Thin Living)

(Meant to be recited aloud rhythmically)

Bip bip bipity bap
that's what you get for saying that ,
Who do you think will ta ake that?,
You cannot talk to me like that,
like that, like that, say what,
like that like that like that

Bip bip bipity bap
act any way you want, talk smack
your hat is really wickity wak
And sense of style so crackity jack
like that, like that, say what,
like that like that like that

Bip bip bipidy bap
I know your momma calls you that
And caters to your every spat
You must think that I take the crack
like that, like that, say what,
like that, like that like that

Bip bip bipity bap,
y'all deserve some pee imp slaps
for raising kids who don't know jack
with no respect and cau-se flack
like that, like that, say what,
like that, like that like that

Bip bip bipity bap
the world's a mess, you must see that
If baby's smoke, 'n' Jake's Kate and stacked
And flicks his booty- right left and back

14

like that, like that, say what,
like that, like that like that

Bip bip bipidy bap
I've said some things, jumped on your back
It is a shame when I attack
but we both have rights to speak, kick back
like that, like that, say what,
like that, like that like that

Bip bip bipity bap
what will be next, I'll tell you what
If we change marriage mom's next, yes Mack
Better believe God will be back
like that, like that, say what,
like that, like that like that

Bip bip bipity bap,
did you just have a heart attack
think I'd turn cheek, not give back
I love you, not your deeds, it is a fact
like that, like that, say what,
like that, like that like that

It is like that, like that, say what
like that, like that like that

Purple

Her beauty is bone deep beyond the patina of her face
Evidence of hues inherited from many a race.
Grace under fire dating back to Eve
Head high despite changes that ebb and leave
Deprivation, injustice, abuse and starvation
honed values delivered when birthing nations
in home spun, flax weave, or cotton.

She should have been in Purple threads
instead of darning, making bread and beds

Mother, you are more royal than you will ever know
This generation from your heritage grows.

You chose well and for life in lifetimes past
raised families that prayed and together did last

His inner fire lit his visage to handsomeness
showing steel backbone stiffened with stubbornness
against hindrances, delays and derailments.
Character and industry he taught with every lesson
respect your elders, authority - God as penultimate

Father, King of men your legacy in Christ perfectly sown
We follow your footsteps seeking to know

Together 50 years plus in a jaded world
Shining stars in night's sea of contempt.
How do we keep bright the torch and wield
it forward making the sheen shy of being unkempt?

Honor Father and Mother and their ways
so your days may be long in the land always

Amber

Beauty is released, they tell me from pressed grapes and tried souls
Like rocks, whose secrets are told by brutal agents which metamorphose.
Boasting glittering crystal arrays, rocks mirror stars whose nuclei burst holes
in the thick recalcitrant darkness. We the encased, thumb our noses
at society, superior in head only, but lie lonely in ivory towers.

Trapped by thoughts, brimming their birthing urn stillborn
a Pandora of pent possibilities endlessly scurry to and fro.
Convinced that the honeyed resin society spits, holds no thorn
some hold to the view 'all is our fault' and we must forego
any attempt to reach beyond personal miasmas.

Internal solitary confinement makes us waking dead
desensitized by deferred detonated dreams. Life becomes drudgery.
Being enrolled in Walter Mitty's retreat we feel lead-
reluctant dogs lashed to a master's will and whim, painful purgatory.
the releasing prayer a cipher still to be found.

Grace lights the way, causing us to admire
hard won capsules of wisdom cooled from fiery throes
of attempts at relationships rife with quagmire.
To be a mosquito in amber long freed of woes,
admired, but untouchable by those who seek gain from our pain

To be a mosquito in amber long freed of thoughts
that like Pandora, whispered probabilities
deferred, and plagued us painfully till wrought
into new ideas, their secrets glittering possibilities
allowing us to defy despair and be touchable, reachable, relatable,
At peace at last, yes, just to be.

Gold

I hold the memory of your laughter at simple pleasures
most close, reliving its bell-like trills
raising my spirit, once 'raggled like storm tamped heather.
You inspired my promise on crimson sunned hills

I will return once more to my home your heart,
bask near the hearth where roaring fires start,
before the last leaf falls.
We'll walk on leaves once more in the gloaming,
the need no more for roaming.

Love is us, complete, sweetly growing.
This promise is true, my vows to you I'll renew
before the last leaf falls.

(Reminiscent of Sting's Fields of Gold)

Pink

Patty cake, Patty cake, star dust man
bake me a snowflake as fast as you can.
A tisket, great task yet Mary masks it
at the ball enshawled. With a fellow, she's dressed in yellow.
She dances nigh to midnight, a modern-day Cinderella

Stepped on a crack and danced with Jack
Mary Mary became quiet contrary when in the garden
Jack picked a rosie, then gave her posy to Suzy Hack
At midnight when woo her he should sweet maiden,
he locked lips with Hack the floozy, leaning on her Cadillac

Patty cake, Patty cake, star dust man
take pseudo dreams and airy fairy tales
which bring only heartbroken wails
sweep them from dustpan to trash can.
Little girls need role models, to discern wills
not false hopes, codependency and sleight of hand.

Rust

She is aloof to the world not out of pride but
fear of cracking, crumbling corroding with pervading guilt
powerless against hands forcing forbidden forays and hurt.
Those hands elicit confusion about pleasures illicit
Then her heart's decay infiltrates deeper past the light
to her tearless, peace-less soul.

He is a brash, fearless, risk taker, causing fights,
foul mouthed the bubbling seething anger is always about
those who should care, but perpetuate travesties under cover of night
their energy only for spirits, smoking, sparring, sparks and shouts.
He raises himself tough, tree against the wind to folk who rain down

slights,
denigrate, pummel, ply with toys then disappear days and nights.

She is the leader of the pack executing daily attacks
on peers who suspect nothing of the blighting within
Home is where soul and self-esteem is stabbed like tacks
pressed into finger tips. Perfection is lined up neatly in little bins
labeled 'this is for your own good', and 'I hope I love you is understood.'
It feels good to kick, punch, make others cry.
A rumor here, teasing there, 'don't hurt nobody' just 'leave em layin' in
blood.
Don't stop till victims lie staring sightless at the sky.

He gets everything he always wanted except their love
and curries favor with peers in order to escape the punches
Set pattern of pleasing, others taking, bought him heart luggage he hove
everywhere, despite desperation heavy as over laden grape branches.
Like the grapes he is ripe for the taking, pulled under
by the roiling current of lust and greed wrapped in affectionate blunder
a boy toy for a boy is born and lives are torn asunder.

She is cold on the street but dare not go back for a coat
at sixteen it already seems lifetimes have passed with every John
who pause only long enough to let her climb in and out
of their cars, too intent on themselves to care about her age.
Dreams take away the stinking reality, if she hadn't run
there might have been foster care, a home, nothing for which to assuage.
Cunningly she charges more than required and bides her time
cleans out a stash, a bus ride to an aunt her out at last

But many are not so lucky, the soil aches from heartrending cries
of the innocents we failed with platitudes,
inadequacies, ignominies and unseeing eyes.
Like Cain we blind wanderers traipse through life's vicissitudes
helpless, powerless, to save those who in early graves lie.
Their blood is on our hands, permanent reminder
of perfidy plain for society to see.
Children are a gift from God not chattel to destroy or broker.

Burgundy

The throb of your heart full with feeling for me
translates to a love language uniquely your own.
I see it in your eyes – thrilled beyond telling when I arrive
and yearning for my return even as I, for a short while will be gone.

Like wine oiling my bones, joy of my life,
I thrive under the reins of your trust.
This hobbling is mutually exquisite
so I want no other tether regardless of the weather.

Although I could not give you fruit from my womb
you rose beyond facts to spiritually renew our vows.
I was brought to my knees by the calm aplomb
you exhibited despite dashed tears you cried that night.
Silent pillowed drops seared the extinction of your name from time
into my memory. But your acceptance erased my defeated bow.

Your fingers often stroke my neck and linger sexily
because you're in tune with me like the jockey
who caresses the horse ridden to take the Triple Crown.
Your euphoria both his and the underdog cresting impossible peaks
to surpass the pack against all odds- climactic finale of dreams owned.
My equestrian, you give me no quarter or coddling.
Your knowing eyes an intentional crop extracting what's inside
for the better of me you and us, yet you stay for the cuddling -
a necessary aftermath.

You chose me and I you.
Because of this we ride hard for US every time

Orange

Street cones lined up in brave neat rows
tell us stridently stay within the lines
while vested cops usher us to the game. The shine
of bright paint gilding my neighbor's girlfriend's toes
distract and remind me of tangerines, mandarins and cuties.
I sit on the nearby bleacher hearing 'play ball,' sipping my smoothie
and listen idly as they giggle at 'hey batta batta, hey'

rolling indolently off the tongue of the citrus toed Susie.

The bright New York logo sitting on cerulean doesn't disappoint
But St Lucie's spring camp is hot and I long for Shea.
In between lulls the swing of her toes creates disjointed
thoughts about the color. Like cotton it splays
through the color wheel weaving twixt the hidden fabric of lives -
Ubiquitously significant but never thriving on its own
as first pick for favorite and I know how it feels.

I yearn to be like Tony, a tiger bellowing 'everything's great!'
but instead, I mirror Nemo searching for love's ache.
A sweet scab of pain to pull at, hoping to sate and slake
myself somehow, somewhere, with someone - a soul mate.
Hiding behind my stripes I must keep swimming,
and fake enthusiasm, stave off cynicism.

Butterscotch, Garfield and Candy Corns are cool
but only in appropriate doses. Harbingers of Fall-
one's high on himself; the others cause Pavlovian drool.
Fast forward through a season full of leaf husks skittering
to and fro, to and fro, echoes of whispers, whispering echoes
morse-ing out a promise of fulfillment, tainting the wind.

Oh the dark places to which one gets indulging in jiggers
of too much of anything especially pity and liquor.
But, I am not a drinker so I pull at the scab again and again.
Watching holiday celebrations blur time till its lost in snowdrifts
I wait till trees and mistletoe sit once again on sidewalks in the rain.

I desire freedom from society's conditioning
but loneliness makes me understand utterly and unequivocally
the essence of prisons most popular pigment. Gleaming
shift up from red those toes bring me back to life's game.
With each clockwork swing I fight against time
striving to own contentment with my maiden name.

But orange is not red, yellow, green nor blue
and Bob's barricades seem destined to keep me from you.
I wake determinedly doggedly seizing each day
forcing positivity into everything I need to say.
Striving for completeness and to know myself
I live moments on my own dance floor not anyone's shelf.

Ubiquitously significant I thrive
on my own just fine, simply glad to be alive.
Warmth and slow released passion hide in pumpkin spice
when one unwraps the secret told by whispering leaves.
Despite the tick of time, to and fro, to and fro, sheaves
of blessing promise love's ache will return with fall.
This wondrous season reveals birth is hidden in death to self.

Parchment and Linen

My letter came back today
a testament of the decay
of our relationship.
I stared at it with teeth chewed lips
wondering how I could let you slip
away in degrees before it was noticeable.

So I draw pen paper and chair
and sit to painstakingly declare
with every stroke and crossed T
what, over the years you've really meant to me
My love is not colossal or epic.
It's shy, sheltered and myopic
but so deep I thought I would drown
rather than let you see it's me you own.

My heart beats against despair's flood
roaring taps mimicking angry broods.
The effort to beat sustained by thoughts of us reunited
I strain to tell you what came before the blighted
remains of us. Pride and fear festered in light's shadow
so silence grew creating our darkened hollow.

The worst filling a couple must face
is loneliness crowding mercilessly between, causing space-
and I put it there because of my fear.
Can you forgive and see your way forward and clear?

I feared you could not unload the baggage
created from manic cougar lovers who were savage.

PTSD from parents and exposure to the street
were rabid guides you used to taunt my innocent
romantic shyness. Things you said slashed my esteem
I was naïve, gullible, so you disparaged my sweet.

I doubted your love forgetting your youth
pride from my pain preventing couth
and I was brutal too. You begged me not to leave
with a dripping deluge of pleas - a roof shedding snow.
But I hoped to force an end to the meanness of those ways
and value the good between us, to change, to stay.

Yet only half the heart remains from desperate cleaves
and instead I stood limned by sunlight at high noon
without you, nary remains of us not even a shadow
while crystal tear tracks cut my cheeks,
mournful monuments my last boon.

I came then finally seeking honest return
but in scarce few weeks you rested in other arms.
Angry, my fingers itched to curl
around your neck and hers- your best friend's ex!
The object lesson I sought to teach turned in a whirl
on its head, and I vexed while you sexed.
Experience shushes hearts into silent submission
so I let the years silently slip away
my only solace she would and could not stay
and I hurt for you. No joy resides in Karma's instant replay

Hated hope led me to try again when you were free
because I ached to bring your love to me
but new life lessons made you execute
a perfect play - player. It seems I was still gullible,
while your heart was hardened, intractable
although you eventually apologized – for what,
abandoning me with no explanation
opening a door for wind to whistle through painfully.

I let you go, sought to live boldly and forget

but life's cruelty crossed our paths to whet
my appetite again and you spoke inveigling words.
I wriggle on your hook suspended halfway
between capture or release. I can't afford
to dangle in such a shameful way. You must sing, say
or snuff us out completely. If I may….

I have no heart to play this way for even one pace
because I don't believe flip flopping should occupy the space
between mature people who have lived, loved
and learned to navigate life's race

I mailed the last letter to you today
you should know I've learned from the years sage
Both of us were wrong in different ways. I write and pray
with insistent pen scratches on parchment pages
about the ending. Before our story
is wrapped in Linen lets blaze a trail
one way or another- no guts no glory.

Carnelian Kaleidoscope Roku

Sleepless, the savagery of your leaving seeps
behind clenched eyelids.
I'm helpless to stem trickling drops
draining steadily across my cheeks
leaden-ing my spirit and spilling onto the sheet.

Facing truth, I'd denied all day so I'd function nary props
I stare at the ceiling blinking hot gravely lids
seeking elusive reprieve wishing there was a way
to change my heart locks or give my feelings SIDS.
My thoughts are crazed inappropriate and wild
love and hate curdle causing a muddled Yin Yang. In dismay
I finally admit this love affair had only one side.

But it didn't feel that way when you'd whisper
honeyed red herrings holding me still for the killing.

After your retreat I staggered, a shadow, listless,
seeking the back side of tomorrow.
Soaked through by false promises- pithily hollow.
I am heavy with the futility of tears.

I cry in and outside yet like Thor' s horror
I can't empty my heart's cauldron today or tomorrow.
It bubbles up Vulcan's best from pain's endless abyss.
Suspended, a bloody phoenix burnt daily - I twist
and turn reborn endlessly on the spit of your spite.

Pain of the heart cripples the body, soul and spirit.
So, I lie here a paralyzed sleeping beauty sans glass box
the waking dreams futile, still born and fragile.
When I think to shatter these 'interminable' locks,
even in my stupor I am determined to ferret
every flaw and falsehood so when I rise,
this nightmare will fade
and I will find myself better, bolder, braver, agile
and free to love someone who is no renegade

Water 1

God like love and water, is the essence of all things
tangible in immersion, the three are equally incorporeal.
Grasp at them jealously they'll flitter to wing
defying attempts at control.
Shaped and colored like the holding vessel
they're selfless, transparent, escaping the pestle
of established order in the world.

We're awed by your power Lucent being of light
in facing torrents of your truth we're overwhelmed
realizing we are non-lucent beings
spirit indwelt thirsty for you at the helm-
This life gives only inklings of the everlasting.

Your love is a force, no a necessity we cannot gainsay
like sparking explosions as sodium wets
or pounding of Pylons before storms calm get.
It catalyzes change, cleanses and reclaims
like water dousing ire, fire, and calming pain
or aiding rust and wearing rock away again and again.
Ne'er failing, You rinse sin's stubborn stains away.

From you we came great Creator-
Our lives are short stories told in timeless trickles
flowing away or back to You -the divine.
Blips in time's wrinkles, we contrarily outlast it.

Breath of heaven fill this thirsting soul of mine
like water fills cells, intimately me entwine
despite my ignorance. I confess I still forget to pray.
When on my knees again I see You are evident
and needed in all my ways,

Heavenly Father you guide my way
quench my thirst, light my soul and me indwell.
Alpha and Omega, Holy Ancient of days.
Creator, breath giver, water everlasting.
You Are; and remain, in everything!!!

Water 2

The love of God constantly pours into my soul
flooding rebellious spaces till they give up their hold
transformed, freed, I point others to you.
River of grace, mercy and blessing up-well from the Holy Spirit
to wear away resistant evil and galvanize me.

Lead me on a new path impossible to travel
without your comfort, conviction, calling and teaching.
Unseen hand guide every step. Lead me.
Let your good news, forgiveness, grace and mercy flow
into all I say and do – a river of blessing for eternity.

<u>Quicksilver</u>

Love, light, breath, and the spirit
All flow and whither they go only God knows.
In all of them the color shows
nothing and concurrently everything.

Love can't be described while feeling it
just as water's flavors are denied when drinking.
Breath is un-capturable while releasing it-
the Holy Spirit indwells yet often overlooked

Love, light, breath and the spirit
Shine on and through me as God purposes
His perfect will is expressed when
my life is yielded and lived for Him

Silver

The color of your eyes in candlelight,
the moon shining on the lake tonight
the flash of steel when blades clash
and glittering tears pearling your lash.

The glint of CD's in the sun,
splashing flashing fish as they run,
the zip of pop tops and fizzle of beer
bobbling Adam's apples, no more is there

The clink unique to coins in pockets
and smash of cymbals dropped harsh in sockets
chained fences struck by wind flung locks
zinc battered by syncopated rain drops

The color of your crucifix and college ring
mercurial emotions subduing will - suffering!
The discord of tines on teeth 'fore swallows
or the kiss of reflecting windshield halos

Tiny 'fish' skittering down spines of books
echo tramping time which robs our looks
despite the slip and slide of gravity's pull
grace's glint appears when hair dulls

Backs bend, gaits slow and eyes dim
wisdom is gained relating with Him
More precious than Gold and Rubies by far
is getting to be athwart the river
So take tucks, dyes, surg'ries, wrinkle relief jars
and give me Faith, sagacity and Silver

Author's Notes

Black

The imagery of Black centers around suffering loss, death and mourning, No one on earth is spared some suffering. Learn its lessons with humility or allow bitterness to set in. When one gives in to bitterness instead of forgiveness darkness swallows the spirit, However, elegance, passion and beauty like no other can be found to reside in the formality of black. Nothing can alter the allure of 'the black dress' a black sports car, a pair of stiletto pumps or well-cut tuxedo.

Green

Life and youth are vibrant and renewing like spring and summer – the seasons of green. Islands around the world show its diverse shades. Contrast this to the busy acquisitive demanding financial world (greenbacks) which can hold us hostage interfering with enjoying life's meaningful pursuits. The author and those she interviewed find joy when they resolve to always engage/view life from a youthful perspective.

Grey

Grey is a space people occupy when romantic relationships go awry or when major life events rock our world. Although it seems empty and misty like clouds the space holds more than one can imagine. People remain in that haunting place until they look into themselves and know what they want, who they are, and embrace necessary change. Other notes – storms of life and the cinders after a fire has burnt itself out.

Red

A complex shade that has many facets; Fires, Fire engines, iconic race cars, War and blood, Christmas, Romance and the heart, Sex, (opening verse allegory to sex embedded), Anger and passion, Beginnings and Endings as seen through sunrises and sunsets,

Commitment and winning in the game of love. Marriage has all of this so it is red to the author.

Yellow

This is another complex shade that can be like green in its energy, refreshment, resiliency and unflinching light. Yet at its darker heart though is cowardice and unfaithfulness juxtaposed against faithfulness – 'Old yeller' vs. 'Yellow bellied'. This ambivalence perhaps was developed when yellow is almost washed out – a paler or untrue version of itself. Yet the true color is as vibrantly constant as the sun. The author explores these in the two relationships described; a toxic abusive one versus one that is reliable and passionate, tender and faithful.

Blue

The newness, refreshing quality of a relationship in which both parties give each other the room to be themselves. When people are lovingly tolerant of each other like the wide openness of the atmosphere and sky, this is reflected in the eternal quality of Blue. The ocean echoes this in its timelessness – shades of eternity, its rhythmic life, cathartic, and soothing power. Flip side of this is the darkness that occurs when the spirit sinks into pain 'the blues' but this journey is a truthful one that leads to cleansing, rebirth and not bitterness because self-evaluation and growth take place in the open 'under the sky' and 'in the ocean.'

White

White is described as the absence of color yet it is blinding in its starkness, revealing power and truth. In Asian culture it is often used for mourning and used in other cultures for death shrouds. But, it also represents celestial beings and holy things. It is really the blending of all colors of the electromagnetic spectrum. Because of this, white is a complex color requiring that its aspects be dealt with in three separate poems.

1 – The blinding void that results when lovers punish each other and are unforgiving during arguments (cold and blistering like a blizzard).

2- The purity in life and relationships when one insists on maintaining a love of life and sacred innocence when regarding others motives and methodologies. The possibilities, that open up for creativity when this is cherished, are invaluable.

3- Christ and the heavenly host and the promise of eternity when we accept and follow him

Lavender

Lavender is a color and an aromatic plant used throughout the ages. In the middle ages and Renaissance, it was especially prevalent in pomanders. Damsels would drop lavender scented handkerchiefs for their lovers to pick up and return to them. It is soothing and not as strident as purple. The author chose a classic old-world style poem to reflect the color. The message is simple and clear. Love is shared privately between two, indwelt with promise and passion and births commitment. It is sweet smelling when pure.

Garnet

This color has a richness deeper than red. Drops of dried blood turn garnet and can be evidence of several things; sacrifice for others wellbeing, ebbing of life, patched wounds, blood bonds. I felt that Christ's sacrifice for us perfectly displays this color.

Copper

Copper is a bright, lustrous, flashy metallic color. The metal is utilitarian and linked to health. I dealt with it in two poems; one showing the versatility of the metal and the other used a bright and playful play on the word in the style of a ballad.

Brown

Brown often reminds us of a favorite teddy bear but yet this color weaves through everything in our lives. This lead me to research shades of brown. The earthy hues are highlighted in bold throughout the poem as they are used. When I began to consider the idea that we come from the earth a discourse on what comprises the human being ensued. Earth has many shades depending on the minerals that are housed within. Earth is volatile in order to bring its minerals to the surface. Humans have three parts; Body, Soul and Spirit. The Body and soul are the most active, physically volatile yet will perish in our physical death while the Spirit's soft voice lives on forever. Incorruptibility encased in the corruptible.

Tin

Tin is a thin silvery metal that when hit sounds almost false as if it did not quite reach its true self. Although it seems playful like one beating on a tin drum this is a harsh discourse. The author looks at society's falling away from age old values to embrace doing whatever they want. Wantonness is not freedom but seems to be confused with it. Questions are asked about how this trend will play out if we continue on the path we have taken. The author makes no apologies as free speech is for everyone.

There are voices on both sides of the fence and in order to have a discussion or argument or inspire thought one must have both sides. But above all Christians are called to love even when they disagree with others. Parents love their children although they must discipline them and tell them the truth if they want them to be well adjusted. God disciplines us with his truths so we can live better lives and experience his blessings - after all He is God. Christians cannot shy away from sharing their faith and telling the truth to others even if it hurts but we must do so in love and with no other agenda than for truth's sake.

Purple

This is a bright, rich but simple color but not a simple poem. True royalty is embodied in our ancestry. The heritage passed down from good parents or our forefathers. We would do well to honor them and the legacy they tried to pass down. We are doomed to repeat history's failures if we don't. We must hold on to character values and pass them down as well. The last note the author maintains is that there is dignity and regality in marriage that lasts a lifetime. Of course, marriage in the biblical sense- the blessed institution begun by God between Adam and Eve).

Amber

Amber is a lovely clear color that can be tinged with green like Peridot, fiery like Copper or golden like Honey. Like honey, it is beautiful but entraps and immobilizes you in its sweet stickiness. Several situations or life conditions can trap us, depression, mental illness, debilitating physical illness, emotional malaise, prejudice, pain, confusion. Life's magical lesson reveals that from pressure and pain in life, endurance, wisdom and inner beauty is born. In order to grow, learn, or change, we must let the cruel entrapping agents do their worst. We must yield (be). We cannot fully appreciate freedom of spirit without first experiencing its opposite. It's how we get there that matters. The storyteller makes their way out of their trapped state (Metamorphoses) when they use the time of their immobilization to learn and weave their thoughts into a positive step ladder leading to freedom. True freedom must be birthed in the mind before physical freedom can be enacted.

Gold

Love's promise to remain true and always return is golden.

Pink

The color for little girls, reminiscent of innocent play, nursery rhymes, hand games, laughter, whispers, cotton candy and fluffy tutu skirts. They are encouraged to wallow in girlish pursuits but often end up dwelling on unrealistic expectations far from reality. But to better equip girls, we need to teach them how to decipher truths and think for themselves. They must know what they want for themselves without waiting for someone to rescue them. Furthermore, they should not enable poor relationships by dwelling in codependency. The trick is to give girls balance between hope and learning to dream and encourage them to strive to achieve those dreams within the context of reality. Also, we must realize that girls can embrace their femininity without having to go overboard to become the brutal, overly dominant, masculinized femme fatale archetype now portrayed in current culture. True womanhood and its strength must be balanced, sensitive and wholly feminine.

Rust

Oxidation causes rust and corrosion when things are exposed too long to air and moisture, then fall prey to it. Children exposed to harmful circumstances crumble too. This sad color is perfect for discussing the blight and decay of injustice to our youth. Children are sexually, mentally, physically, emotionally abused and traumatized by our harsh selfishness. They are bullied and pimped out and the result is a crumbling of spirit and society as told by this poem. Some do make it to adulthood and are redeemed or reborn so they do not perpetuate the cycle but others fall victim and perpetuate it. Rust is a sad moratorium on the fact that if we don't fix things society will crumble. When we damage children, we damage our future.

Burgundy

There is richness to a love that can surpass obstacles which would take out lesser people: such as loss of a child or the inability to have a child. Finding new dreams to share together and being able to move on, is testament to the depth and richness of the deep love that can be found in some human spirits.

Orange

This color, cusp between red and yellow signifies what happens when society conditions others to marry or else be considered less than. It puts people into prisons feeling unfulfilled and lonely. The color is used for prison garb and so the author plays on this theme throughout the poem even while discoursing on other things/ images related to the color. There is also hope which whispers from within the orange tinge of a sunrise. The cycle of Sunsets signal ending of days and sunrises, counterpoints Fall and winter in the rhythm of seasonal changes. These two examples illustrate the necessary death to self (of days/tree leaves in winter) which aids rebirth – (in mornings and spring). The message is not to be too caught up in the self and one's own pain but die to self so one can look outward and be reborn – this helps yourself and others.

Parchment and Linen

These two colors are used for wedding invitations, love letters in ancient times, recording history in scrolls, clothing for royalty and death shrouds. This discourse traces this theme through the course of a lover's tale of love for their sweetheart that has taken a lifetime to die. Several junctures in life where hope for the love to rekindle occur and each time it dies a mini–death till the final realization occurs; it will never be reborn.

Carnelian Kaleidoscope Roku

As the wheel turns in a kaleidoscope the multifaceted patterns and images change. The bleeding heart trying to heal after a break up is fickle, turns on a dime and causes muddled patterns of thought alternating with moments of self-discovery, and clarity. Roku pottery often has a kaleidoscopic appearance. This poem journeys with the suffering lover who finds the way back to themselves carrying hard won truths.

Water

1) Its often said that God is love, God is spirit, God births our spirit and His spirit indwells believers. God is Omniscient, Omnipresent, Omnipotent, yet despite all this it is very hard to describe God in a tangible way. One really cannot fully understand or know God with the mind. The only way to clarity of any kind is through faith (immersing oneself in Him totally in your spirit) - believing. The same thing occurs with water. We cannot describe it or know it unless we drink or immerse ourselves in it. Take a chance and indulge the author's allegory as she states respectfully (without being irreverent in any way), that God is like water – in everything, vital for everything yet escapes true definition.

2) God's love flows through us to others like water in our universe.

Quicksilver

Quicksilver is a dark silver color used as a synonym for mercury. Its nature is changeable and hard to grasp or contain. The author revisits the fact that only after finding a vessel for it to be poured into, i.e. yielding to its nature, then its true nature is revealed.

Silver

Silver has a beautiful blinding sheen one can tolerate in flashes of glances. The author uses snippets of phrasing to represent images seen in flashes as they appear or stem from silver. The aging process (silver grey hair) and development of wisdom is precious like the metal and gains its value when a price is paid (youth and living) . Faith in God and knowledge of him makes a life precious in his sight. The poem ends with the statement that gaining these things is more worthwhile than the temporary things the world can offer.

Acknowledgements

I would like to thank God first and foremost for blessing me so magnanimously and for giving me the opportunity to share my voice. He has inspired my meditations, thoughts and creativity. Life has many chapters, seasons and moods. I have found a strong Faith makes all the difference. Every day the beauty and truth of His word uplifts and astounds me.

I would also like to thank my family, friends, and special people whose conversations with me allowed 'Color Me'. As you shared your life lessons and thoughts, the color of the experience became vivid, relevant and touched the heart. You have given me the moments, the flashes of light which birth poems. For this, to you all, I am forever indebted.

www.ingramcontent.com/pod-product-compliance
Lightning Source LLC
Chambersburg PA
CBHW061758040426
42447CB00011B/2356